SOLO GUITAR

GAME OF THRONES™

ORIGINAL MUSIC FROM THE HBO® TELEVISION SERIES

Arranged by Jeff Jacobson

ISBN 978-1-5400-5924-6

HAL•LEONARD®

Visit Hal Leonard Online at
www.halleonard.com

Contact us:
Hal Leonard
7777 West Bluemound Road
Milwaukee, WI 53213
Email: info@halleonard.com

In Europe, contact:
Hal Leonard Europe Limited
42 Wigmore Street
Marylebone, London, W1U 2RN
Email: info@halleonardeurope.com

In Australia, contact:
Hal Leonard Australia Pty. Ltd.
4 Lentara Court
Cheltenham, Victoria, 3192 Australia
Email: info@halleonard.com.au

Game of Thrones

By Ramin Djawadi

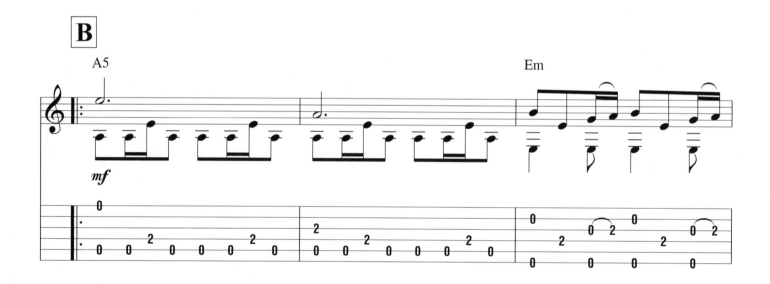

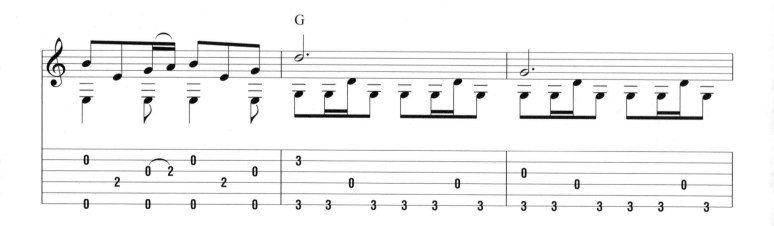

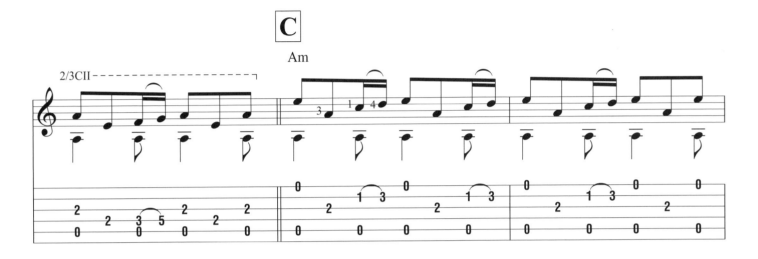

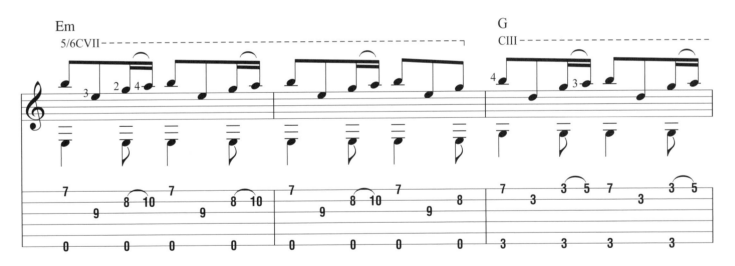

The Children

By Ramin Djawadi

Drop D tuning:
(low to high) D-A-D-G-B-E

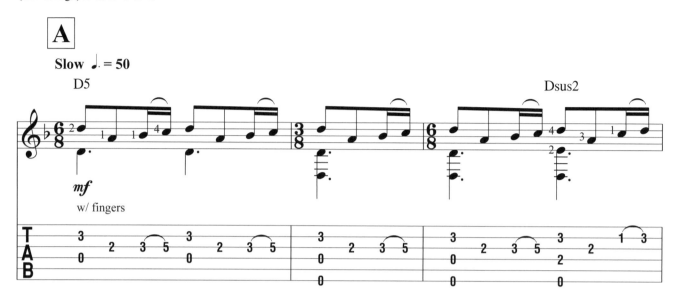

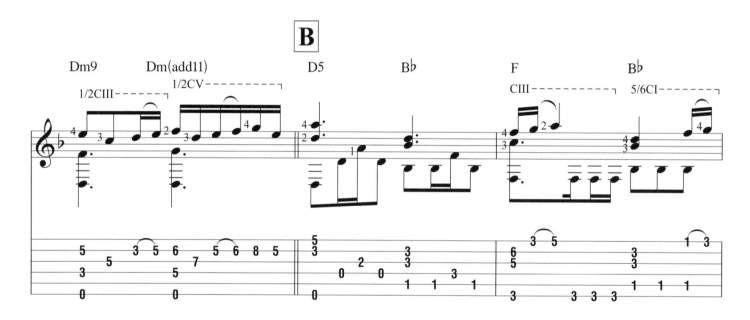

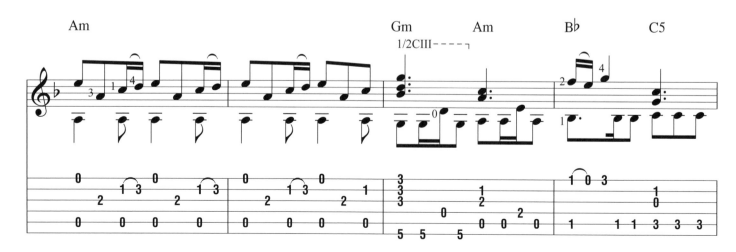

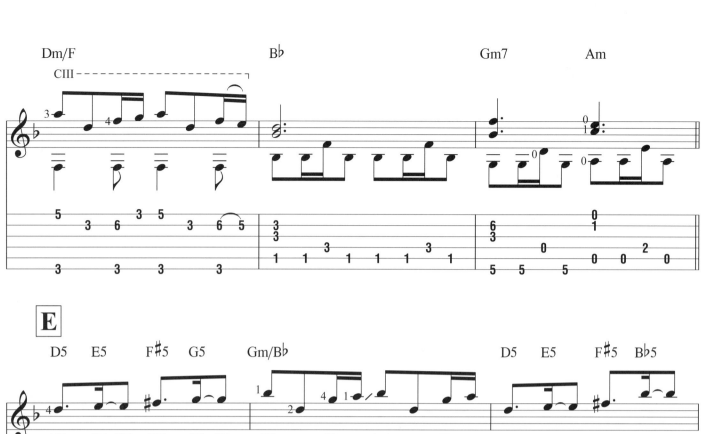

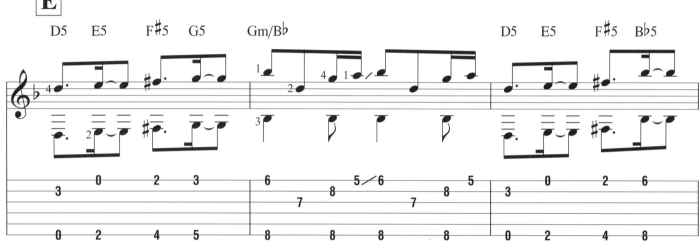

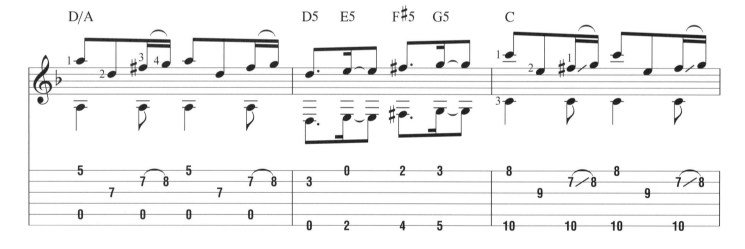

Goodbye Brother

By Ramin Djawadi

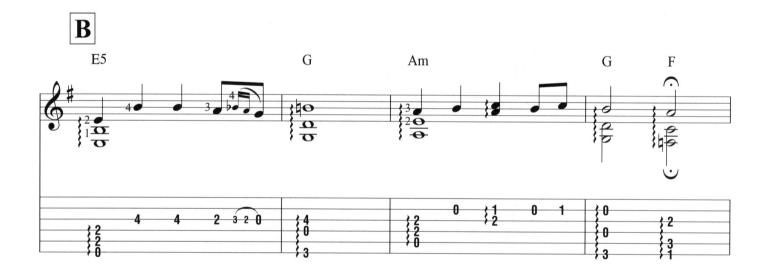

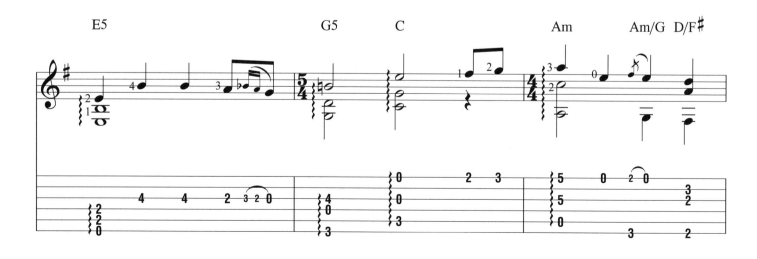

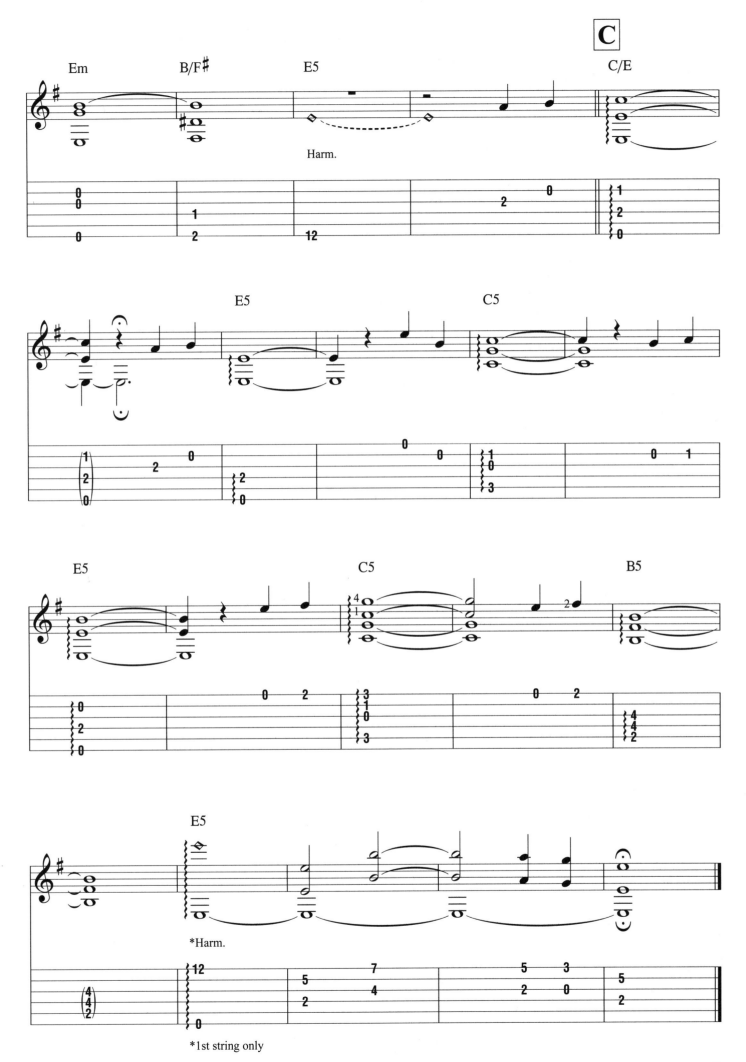

The Bear and the Maiden Fair

By Ramin Djawadi and George R.R. Martin

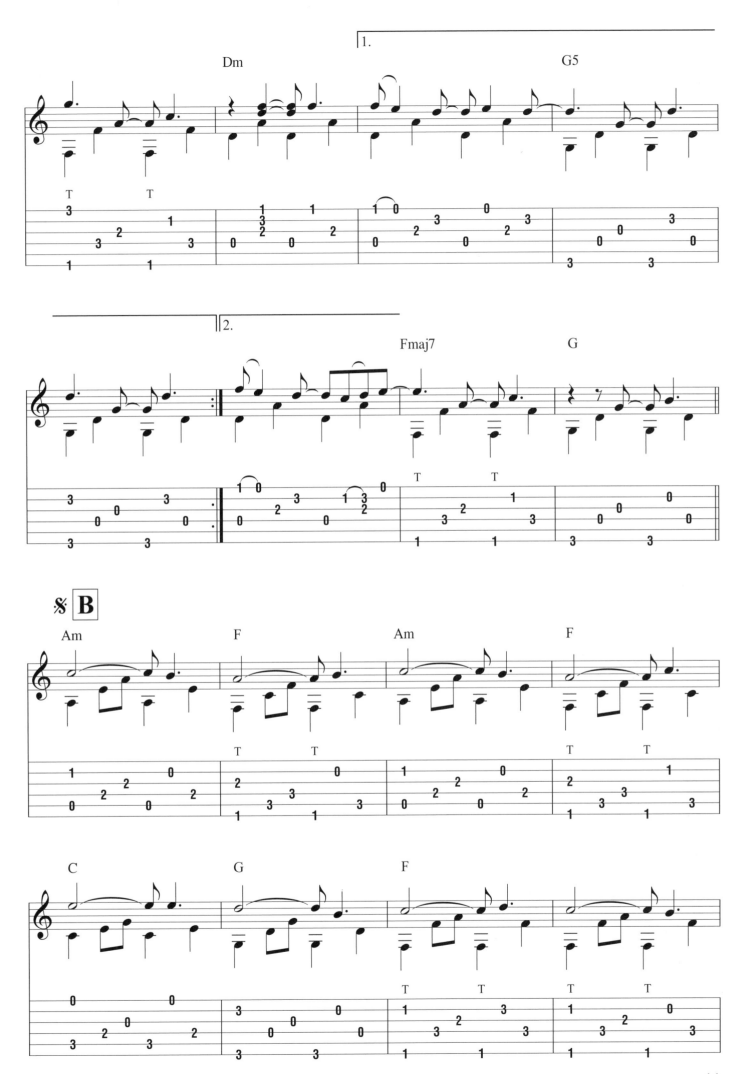

To Coda 1 ⊕

To Coda 2 ⊕

C

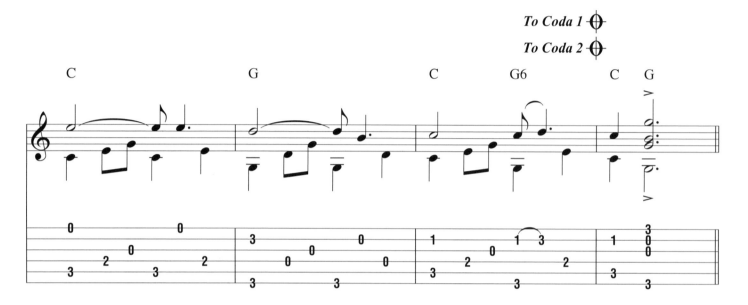

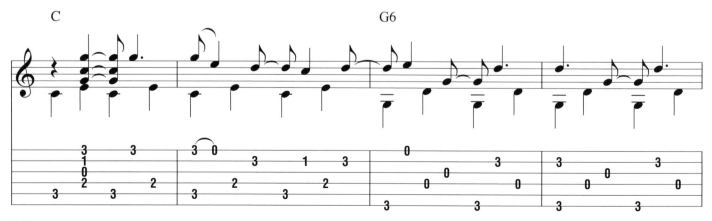

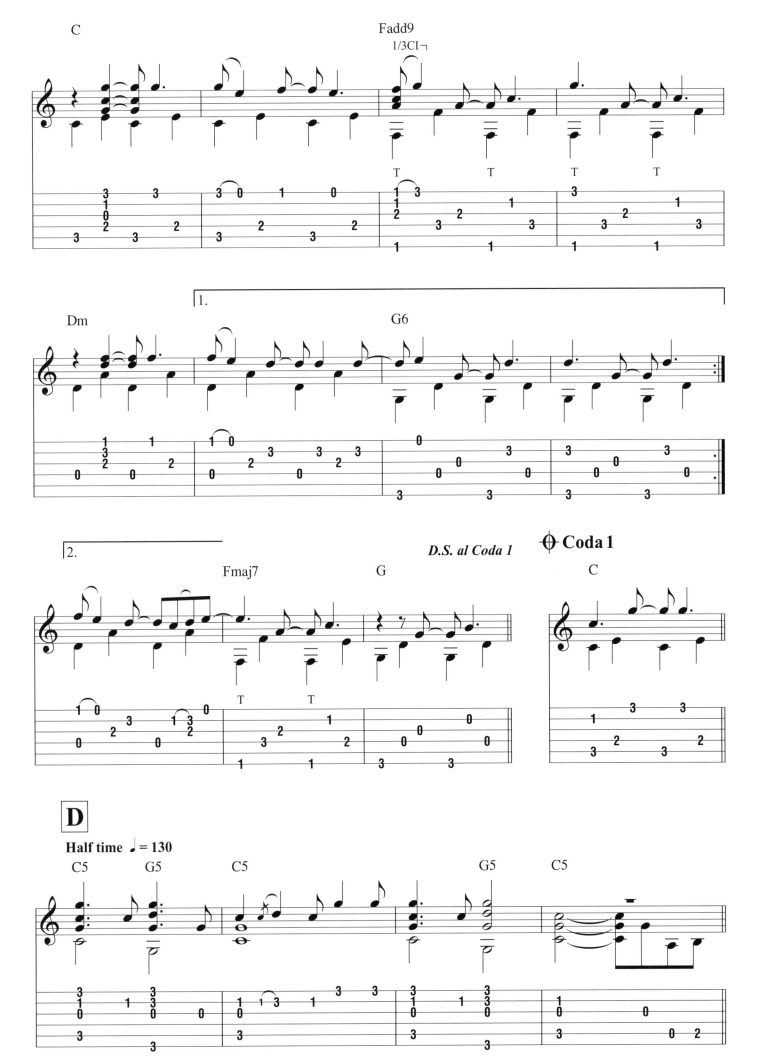

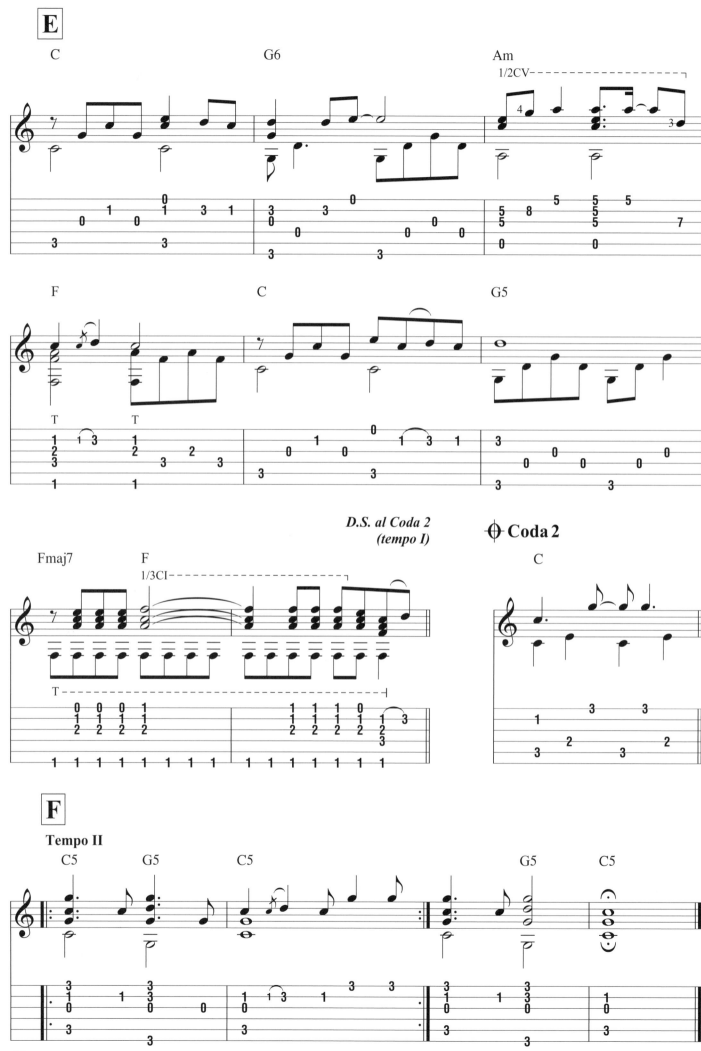

14

A Lannister Always Pays His Debts

By Ramin Djawadi

Drop D tuning:
(low to high) D-A-D-G-B-E

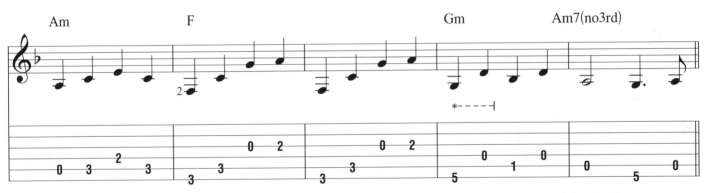

*Let low G ring through beat 2 only.

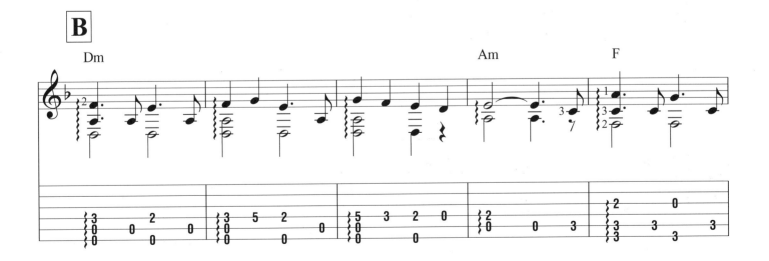

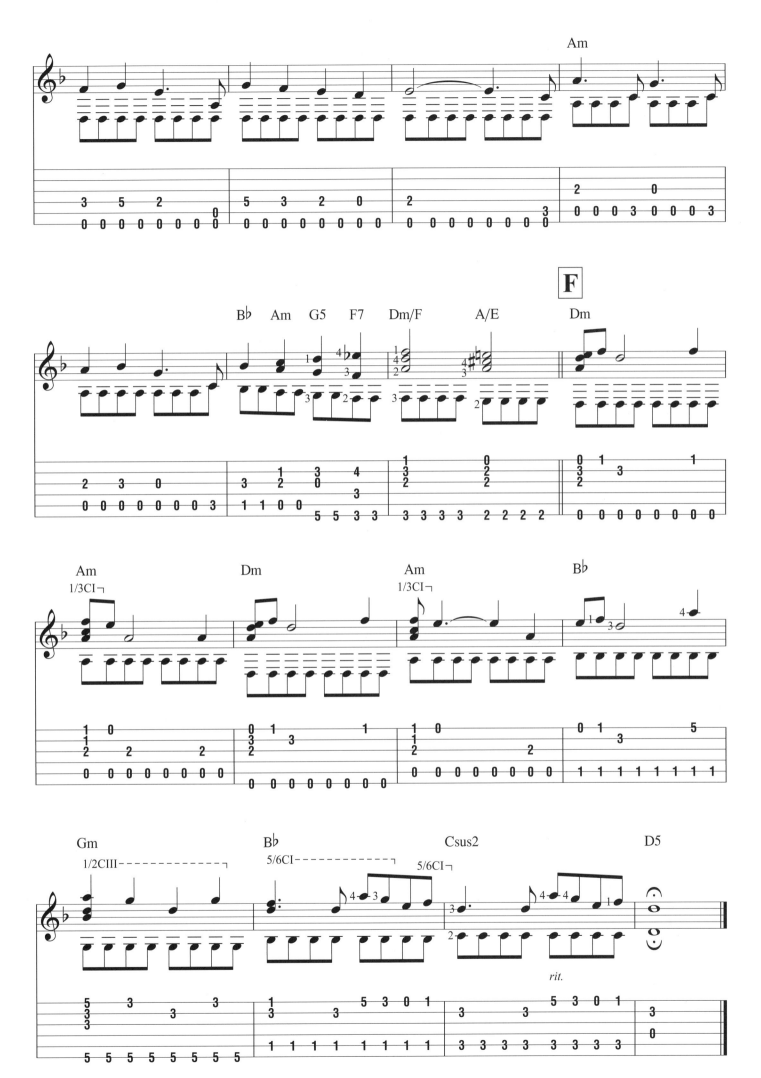

Light of the Seven

By Ramin Djawadi

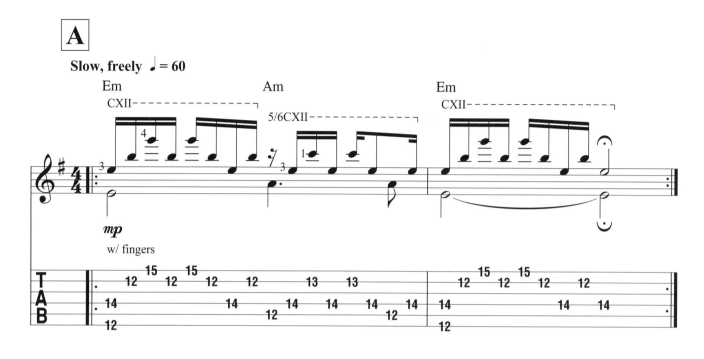

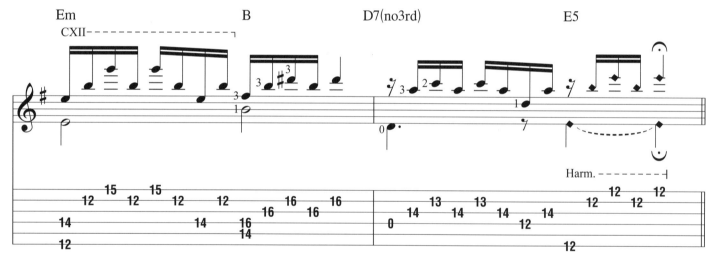

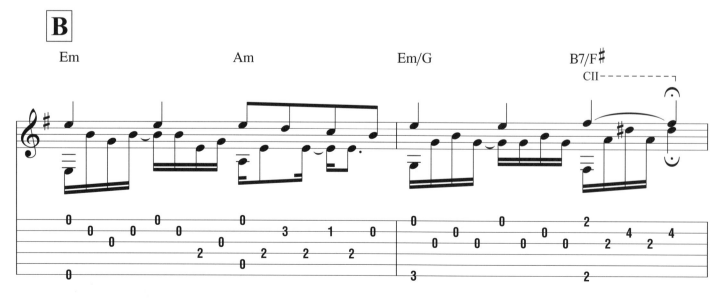

*Refers to upstemmed notes only.

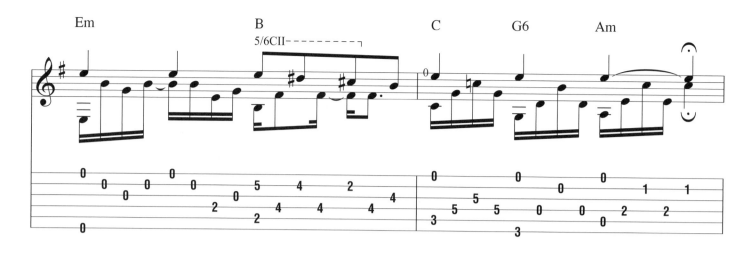

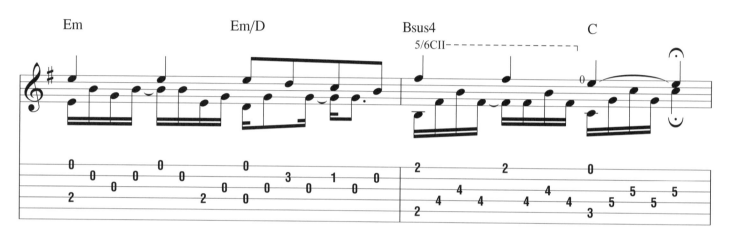

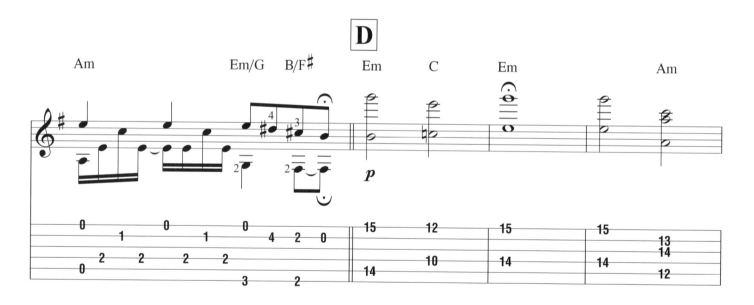

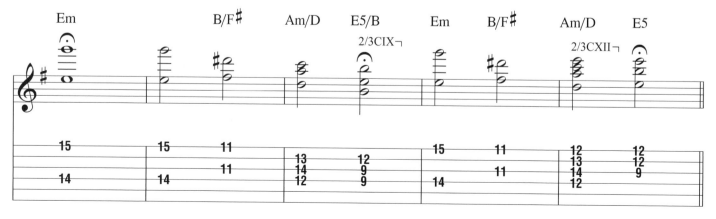

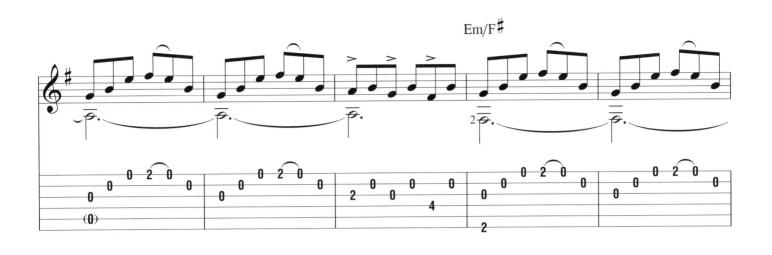

Em/F#

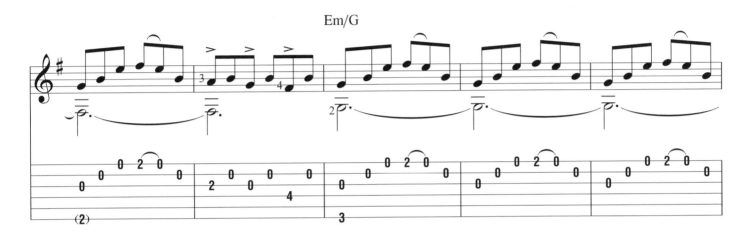

Em/G

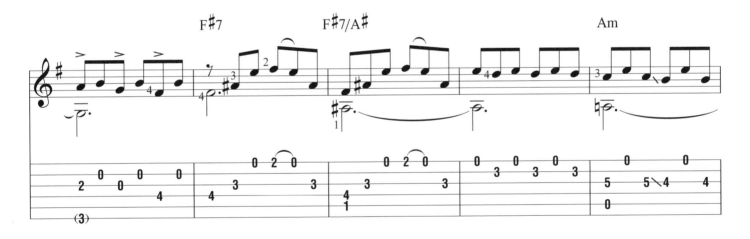

F#7   F#7/A#   Am

G

E5

Mhysa

By Ramin Djawadi

Drop D tuning:
(low to high) D-A-D-G-B-E

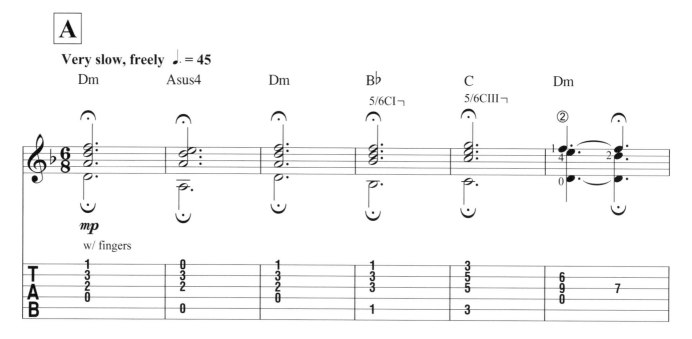

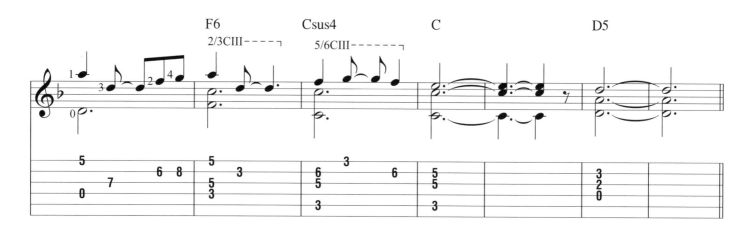

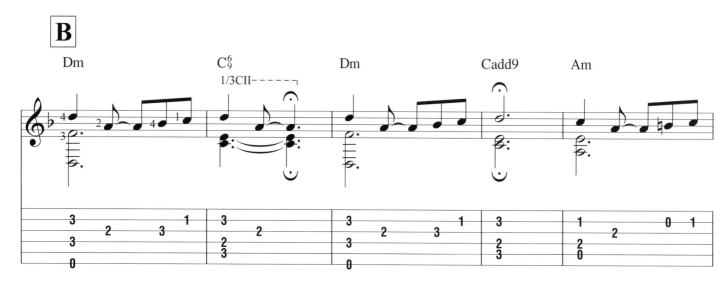

**Refers to top note only.

*Rapidly strum w/ thumb.

Throne for the Game

By Ramin Djawadi

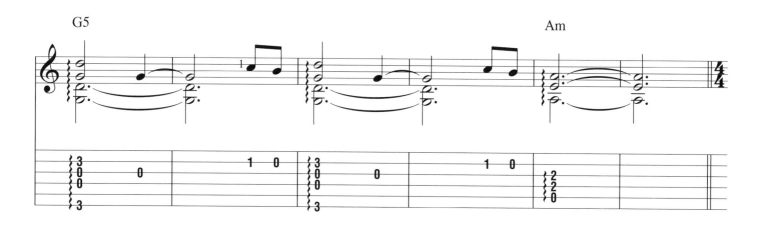

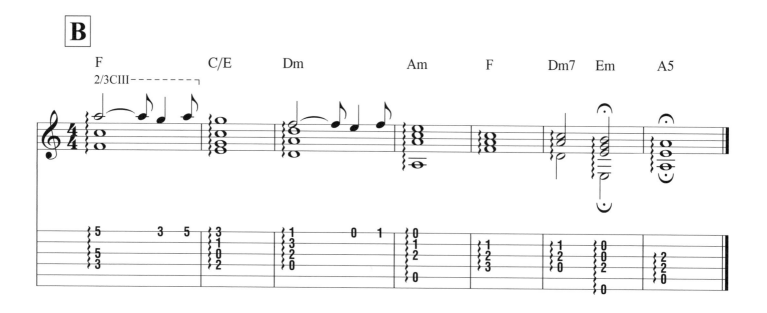

The Rains of Castamere

Words and Music by Ramin Djawadi and George R.R. Martin

Tuning:
(low to high) E-G-D-G-B-E

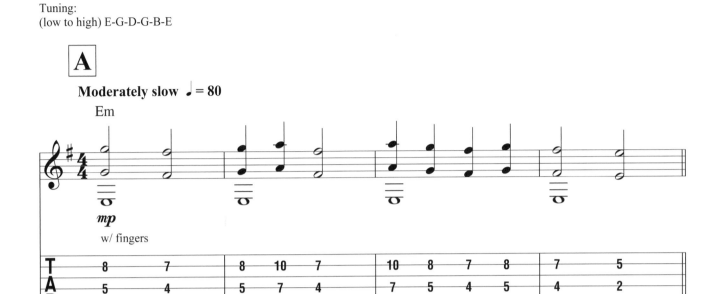

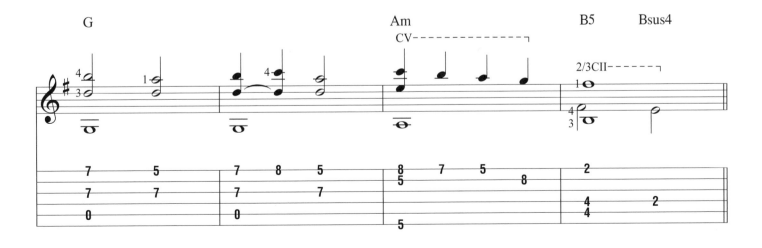

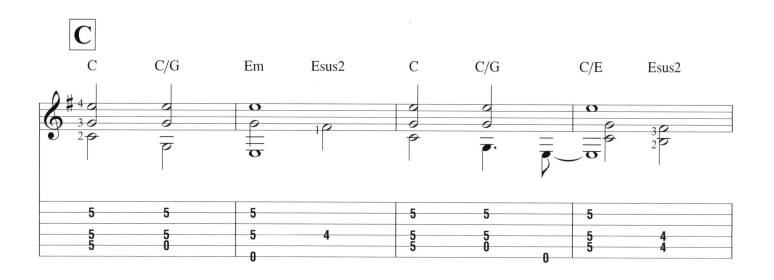

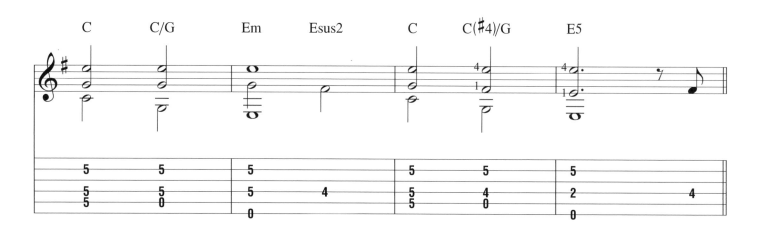

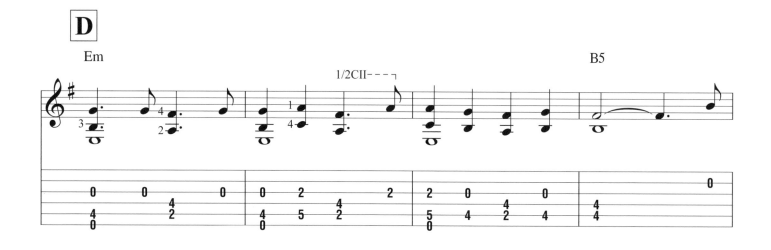

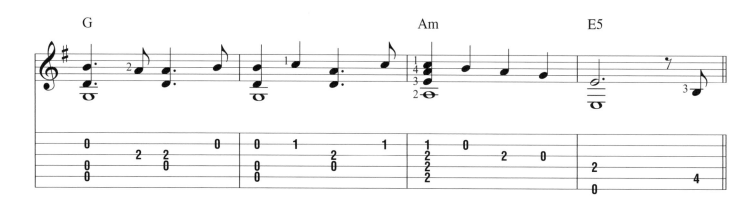

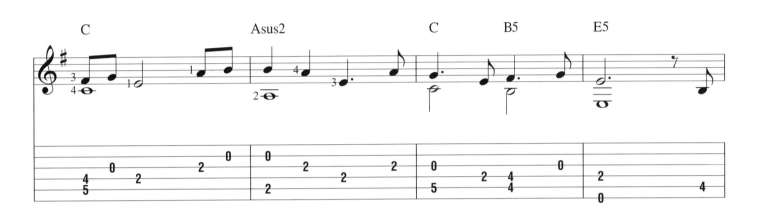

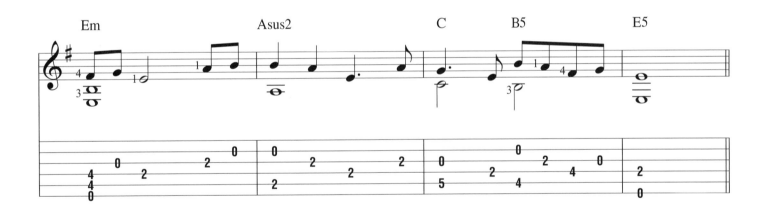

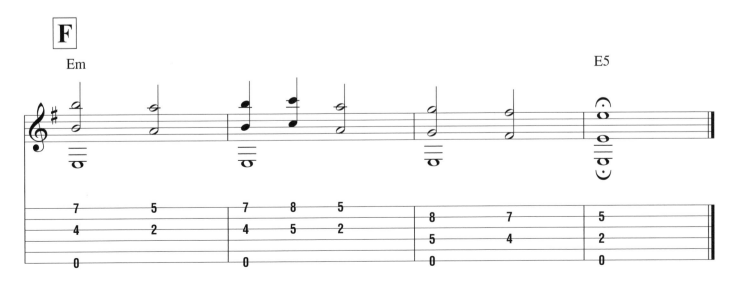

The Winds of Winter

By Ramin Djawadi

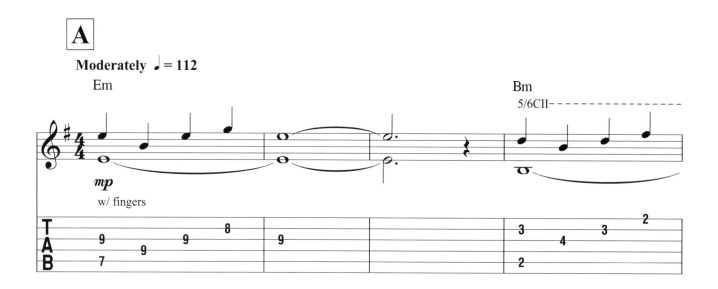

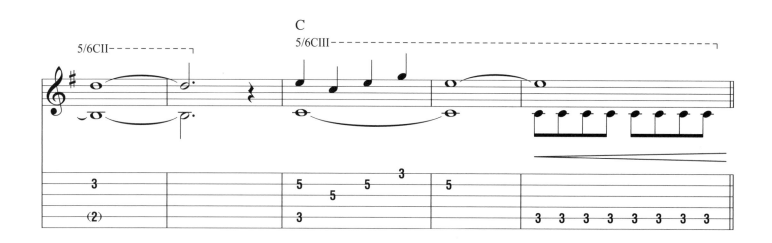

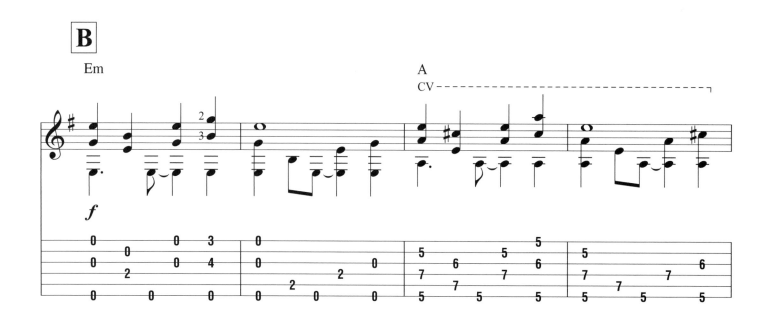

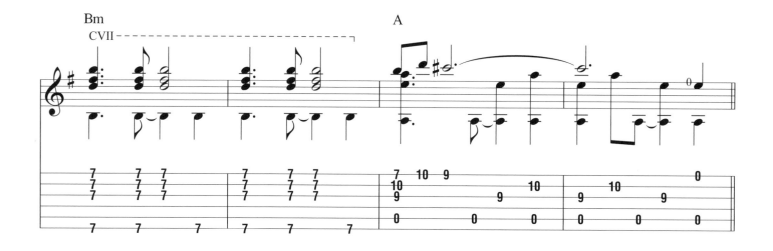

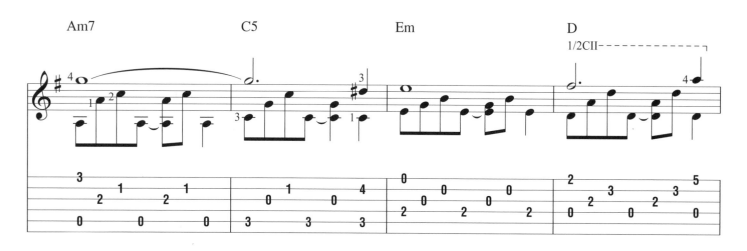

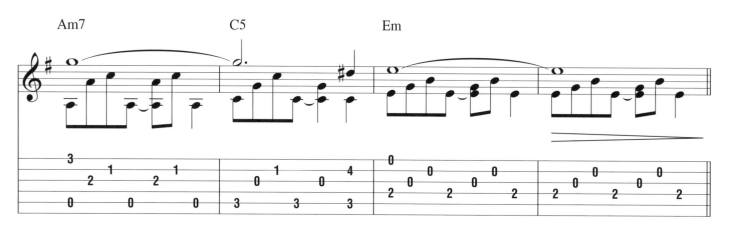

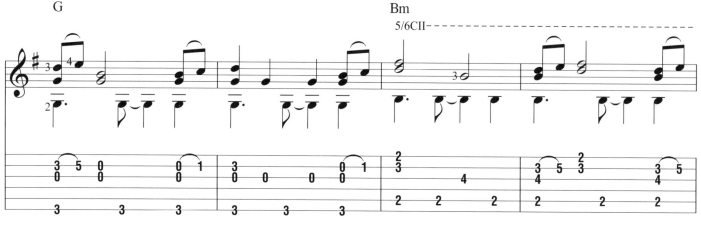

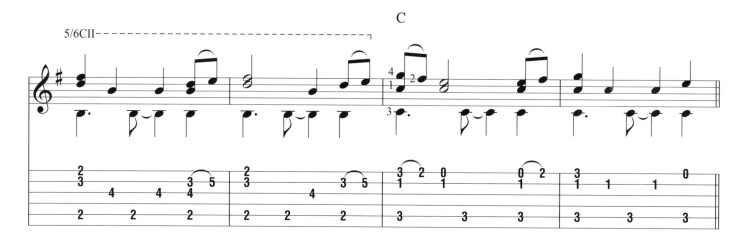

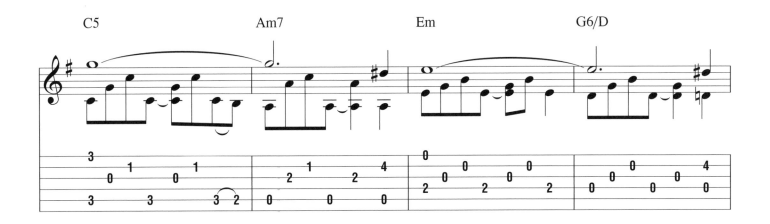

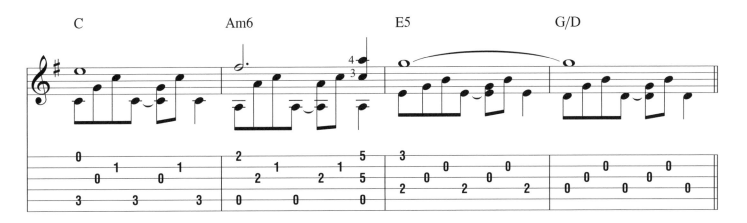

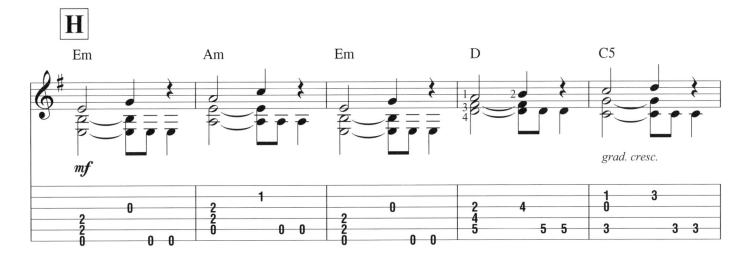

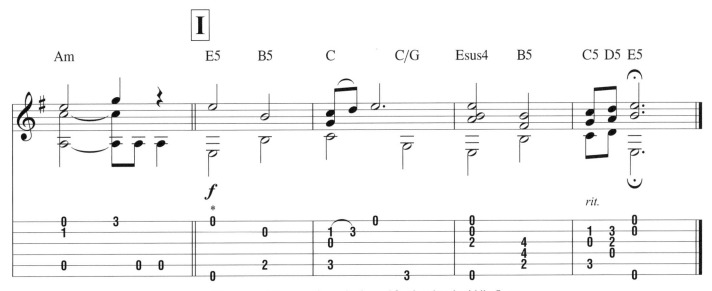

*Stop open 5th string from ringing w/ fret hand and middle finger.

Finale

By Ramin Djawadi

Drop D tuning:
(low to high) D-A-D-G-B-E

A

Slow ♩. = 50

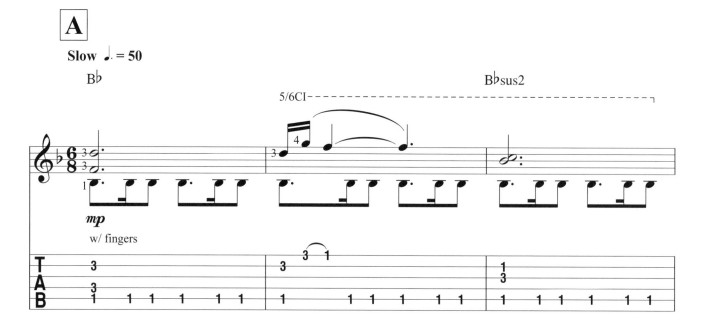

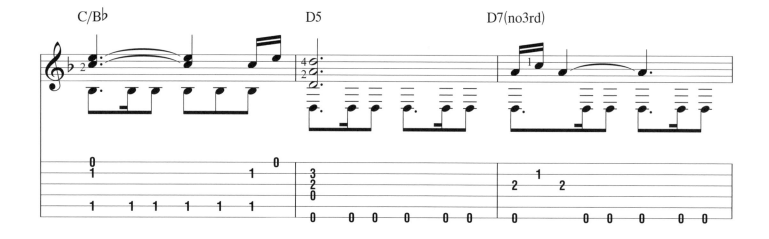

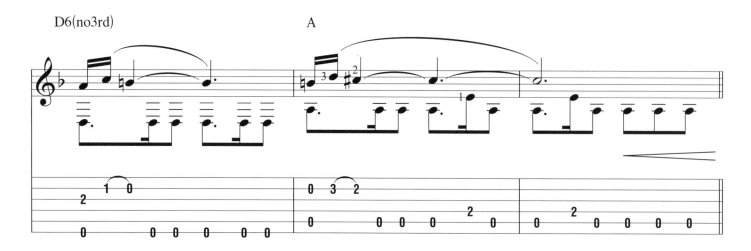